The Accurate Price Guide

for Miniature Lamps I and II

by Ruth E. Smith & Helen A. Feltner

Showing unlisted photographs of lamps

1469 Morstein Road, West Chester, Pennsylvania 19380

CLASSIFICATION GUIDE

As in all collectibles, there are many miniature lamps that must be set apart from the more ordinary examples because of their scarcity and workmanship. We have, therefore, assigned the following code to establish our ratings of those lamps:

(S) Scarce
(R) Rare
(VR) Very Rare
(NA) Not Available

As more and more lamps come to light (no pun intended), we are finding that *no* book can be considered *the* complete and unabridged reference source on the subject. The fact that we continue to discover "new-old" specimens gives impetus to the collector to carry on in the quest for lost treasures. As witness to the worth of the continuing search, such booty as the "Little Crown", a three-inch iron stemmed, glass font mini-lamp (ca. 1877) has surfaced. Likewise, a "Regal Fancy Panel" clear stem lamp made by the Riverside Glass Company of Wellsburg, West Virginia and a Findlay "Feathered Arch Font-Triple Stem" clear miniature have emerged. Needless to say, these lamps do not fall into the normal range of stem lamps and must be classified as Very Rare and priced accordingly, i.e., Little Crown, $325; Regal Fancy Panel, $135; Feathered Arch—Triple Stem, $150. (also known as the Dakota lamp).

We hope that you enjoy The Accurate Price Guide for Miniature Lamps I and II. We will send a free catalog upon request. Write to: Schiffer Publishing, Ltd., 1469 Morstein Road, West Chester, Pennsylvania 19380.

Printed in the United States of America.
Published by Schiffer Publishing, Ltd.
ISBN: 0-88470-142-2

Price Guide
for Miniature Lamps I

Acknowledgments

We, the authors of this updated price guide feel a professional and ethical obligation to our many friends, who are esteemed collectors and dealers in miniature lamps, to substantiate the authenticity of lamps listed in this price guide.

Both collectors and dealers must demonstrate prudence and caution in purchasing miniature lamps. All published information in Frank R. and Ruth E. Smith's *Miniature Lamps Book I,* and *Book II,* is based on years of exhaustive research, intensive study, and close examination of miniature lamps. However, the author assumes no responsibility for counterfeit purchases. The updated SMITH/FELTNER PRICE GUIDE is an instructor, and should not function as an only resource for determination and value. It is hoped that this communication will clarify any refutable information published in *Miniature Lamps Book I,* and *Book II and also the Price Guide.*

We, the authors of this updated price guide are happy to add unlisted photographs of miniature lamps that have not been photographed before to this updated price guide. We wish to thank the following collectors in allowing us to show photographs of their unlisted lamps. Marjorie Hulsebus, Glendale, California; Nedra Lennox, Adrain, Michigan; and John Ness, York, Pennsylvania.

Foreword

Since the publication of our first price guide, much has transpired in the miniature lamp field of collecting. Inflation has struck! Newcomers are rushing in to INVEST. Is nothing sacred? Must a once-tranquil pastime be turned into a frenzied fiasco of "Buy Low — Sell High"? We should hope not. In truth, no one wants to lose money. We would all hope that our collections will someday reflect the wisdom of our purchases. And who will deny what a distinct "high" is felt when we do, indeed, "Buy Low"? However, these days appear to be slipping away from us and may soon become as aberrant as some recent auction prices.

In making adjustments in guide prices, we have applied information gleaned from show prices, auctions (some too high, some too low), dealers and individual collectors. Many factors must be considered in each instance, i.e., you may see a lamp at a show or shop which is priced at $525, but, upon discussion with the dealer, you may actually purchase it for $450, reflecting a variance of $75. An auction price results from two or more persons, desiring a particular lamp, going toe-to-toe in many instances, whereas less avid bidders have long-since dropped out of the contest having decided enough is enough.

With individual collectors, personal preference sets the price. The guide may quote a price that is somewhat lower or higher, as the case may be, than the value it may represent to one who specializes in collecting this particular category of lamps. We stressed before, and we stress again, that you, the collector, must determine your own limits. Our prices are intended to portray a median from which to negotiate and to substantiate insurance evaluations. The rest is up to you. Good luck and happy hunting!

Introduction to Book I

This price-guide quotes the average prices of the current retail prices of Miniature Lamps in book I and book II.

We have endeavored to make prices as accurate and up-to-date as possible. Prices on lamps have been compiled from all available sources such as Auction Houses, Antique Shows, and Dealers. Prices quoted also depend on the abundance, scarcity, and also the condition of the lamps. A few are sometimes found with small chips on the shades which is to be expected, but large cracks and chips will lower the price drastically. In different parts of the country prices vary and due to the fast rise in inflation present prices vary considerable.

Over the years many miniature lamps have been reproduced, and some new ones made. These reproductions are pretty and hard to tell from the originals and collectables in themselves as well as the new ones and they should not be priced or sold as old or the original ones. The best protection against acquiring a reproduction miniature lamp and paying for the original is to buy only from a reputable dealer. The dealer will have many years of experience in the field, however, this does not mean a dealer himself cannot make an error but chances are greatly reduced. A reputable and ethical dealer will always stand by what he sells.

Each lamp has a number in the price-guide which corresponds to the numbers in the Miniature Lamp book I and II. All one has to do is find the lamp number in the books and compare numbers to numbers in the price-guide for the price.

All prices quoted on Miniature Lamps are in book I and book II, and are intended to serve only as a "Guide" and not warranted as to accuracy as prices change so fast. No responsibility, liability, losses, or other errors incurred by the buyer, seller or anyone else using this price-guide will be assumed by the writers as well as the Publishers of this price-guide for Miniature Lamp books I and II.

I As pictured 510.00R
Also known to have been made in
cranberry and other colors without
decorations, which lowers price
considerably 260

II 1st lamp, left 340S
2nd lamp, center 535S
3rd lamp, right 435S

III 1st lamp, purple/gr.m.gl 295
2nd lamp, lavender satin 1075R
3rd lamp, pink satin 645S
4th lamp, red satin 525S
5th lamp, amber satin 750S
6th lamp, yellow/green m.g. . . . 295
Note: Not pictured, these lamps also
came in light blue and green
satin 650S

IV Pink cased glass 4800VR
1 Whale oil 280R
2 Whale oil 175S
3 Clear finger 175S
4 "The London Lamp," clear 80S
"The London Lamp," green 100S
5 "Handy," clear 50
"Handy," light blue, cobalt, green,
pink, frosted 80
6 "Firefly," clear finger 125
7 "Little Firefly," with handle and
original shade 160S
"Little Firefly," without
handle 160S
Note: A plainer version has been seen in
a cast metal holder 195R
8 "Little Firefly" chandelier 2250VR
9 "Little Firefly," milk glass 245S
10 Pink, white bristol 245S
11 Both lamps come in varying colors of
milk glass and transparent glass
stems 325S
12 "Evening Star," clear with
handle 125S
"Evening Star," clear without
handle 125S
13 "Little Harry's Night Lamp" . . . 145S
14 "Little Harry's bracket lamp . . . 1000VR
15 "Little Harry's Night Lamp"
clear 110S
"Little Harry's Night Lamp,"
cobalt 185R
16 "Little Favorite" left 135S
"Little Beauty" right 135S
17 "Little Harry's" milk glass
stem 260S
18 Cranberry, silver base 520VR
19 "Little Twilight" clear 190S

20 Improved Banner, clear 85
Improved Banner, milk glass 95
21 Clear glass, red paint 75S
22 Noxall, clear 110S
Noxall, milk glass 145S
23 Time Lamp 210
24 Milk glass 150
25 Bristol 155S
26 Blue Bristol 135S
27 Metal base 135S
28 Blue, green opalescent 150S
29 Nutmeg, clear 45
Nutmeg, milk glass 70
Nutmeg, blue, green, cobalt 90
30 Manila, clear, milk glass 95S
Manila, cobalt, green, amber . . . 110S
31 Brass saucer 50
32 Little Duchess, clear 110S
Little Duchess, milk glass,
blue 135S
33 Blue, green, amethyst 100S
V Left 3500VR
Middle 3300VR
Right 3250VR
VI Bisque Indian 7000VR
VII Santa Claus 2800S
VIII Cameo 5550VR
IX Left, MOP satin 2000VR
Right, candy stripe 1200R
X Left, painted milk glass 365S
Right, Elephant 2250VR
XI Cranberry 1350VR
34 Amber cup and saucer 175S
Clear cup and saucer 110S
35 Amber 175S
Clear 125S
36 Blue, green amber, cobalt,
amethyst 110
Clear, frosted 75
Cobalt without handle 125S
37 Clear 135S
38 Spatter glass 200S
39 Milk glass with painted
designs 110
40 Blue, white, cranberry 325
41 Crystal, without matching
shade 75S
42 Clear 135S
43 Milk glass 160S
44 "Little Jewel" clear 90S
"Little Jewel," green 125S
45 Clear 75S
46 Blue, amber picket pattern 150S
Vaseline 165R
Stem, not shown, clear, amber,

blue 135S
47Amber, blue 145S
48Clear base with cranberry
    shade 85
    Green with green shade 95
49Blue paneled glass 150S
50Log Cabin, amber, blue milk
    glass 625S
    Log Cabin, clear . . . 350.00 . . . 695S
    Log Cabin, blue opaline 775S
51Shoe, clear 425S
    Shoe, blue, amber 800S
52Match-holder, amber, blue,
    milk glass 650S
    Clear glass 425
53Milk glass, white, blue 45
54Milk glass 85
    Milk glass, blue, custard 100
55Left, clear 75
    Right, with matching shade,
    green, amber 150S
56White milk glass with
    reflector 110
    Blue milk glass with reflector . . . 145
57Blue, white milk glass 125S
58Cobalt with mirror reflector 75
59Brass with reflector 75
60Tin hanging lamp 65
61Tin, painted red or green 65
62Lockwood Nickel lamp 400VR
63Lockwood lamp label . . . . NA
64Acme reflector lamp 75
65Brass reflector lamp 95S
66As shown, with shade 145S
67Brass plated, no shade 75
68Pewter with or without gilt 90
69Brass boudoir lamp with
    shade 125
70Brass finger lamp 75S
71Pottery "Genie" lamp 75
72Nickel Aladdin-type 85
73Brass hinged pedestal 65
74Brass hinged in bracket position . . 65
75Crystal Aladdin 375VR
76Brass pedestal, swinging font 75
77Beauty Night Lamp 85
78Nickel "Comet" 95
79Brass Barrel 250VR
80Brass Fire Engine 1150VR
81Brass spice lamp 650R
82Brass Sleigh 675S
83Student lamp 1500VR
84Single student 675S
85Single student 575S
86Double student 525S

87Double student 825R
88Double student 1275R
89Double student 1275R
90Brass weighted, with reflector . . . 385VR
91Bracket lamp 365R
92Nickel "Ray-O" 235S
93Copper lamp 50
94Tin lamp 15
95Brass lamp 110
96Peg lamp 300S
97Jeweled shade, brass 115
98Brass, jeweled shade 300S
99Candleholder 275
100Brass base 285R
101Brass, green milk glass shade . . . 185S
102Brass pedestal 185S
103Clear stem 60
    Clear stem, frosted font 75
104Clear 65
    Amber, blue 95
105Clear 60
    Blue 85
106Clear (Octavia) 75
    Green, amber, blue 110S
107Clear 85S
    Clear stem, frosted font 115S
108Clear 100
    Green 145
109Green 275S
    Clear 180
    Frosted font 235S
110Bullseye, clear 45
    Bullseye, red or blue flash 60
    Bullseye, clear with painted
    flowers 60
    Bullseye, frosted with painted
    flowers 80
    Bullseye, milk glass, green amber,
    amethyst, blue 110
111Blue, amber, green, milk glass . . 125
    Clear 90
112Amber, blue, green, milk glass . . 125
    Clear 90
113Clear 90S
114Green, blue, clear stem-frosted
    font 135S
    Clear 95S
115Clear glass-frosted font 130S
    Clear 95S
116Fish scale blue, green, amber,
    vaseline 135S
    Clear 100
117Amber, blue, teal 125S
    Clear 85S
118Clear 100

Vaseline blue amber 165S
119 Clear 18
120 Clear 105S
121 Acorn, no shade as shown in
    book—crystal. 65
    Gold or silver mercury, milk
    glass 110
122 Milk glass 50
123 Milk glass 50
124 Milk glass salt shaker lamp 180S
125 Christmas lamp, milk glass 150
    Christmas lamp, clear glass 135
126 Milk glass 150S
    Clear glass. 125S
127 Clear glass. 150
    Clear with frosted panels 195S
128 Milk glass 135
129 Milk glass 195
130 Milk glass 190
131 Clear glass. 105
    Milk glass 135
132 Clear 115
    Milk glass 135
133 Clear 115
    Milk glass 135
134 Clear 115
    Milk glass 135
135 Clear 115
    Milk glass 135
136 Clear 175S
137 Clear 185S
    Milk glass 200S
138 Clear 125
    Light and emerald green 160
139 Clear or painted clear 100
    Milk glass with painted flowers . . 200
140 Painted clear glass 135
141 Clear embossed glass, painted 160S
142 Clear or painted clear 75
143 Any or all combinations. 75
144 Clear Westmoreland 275S
145 Clear Westmoreland pedestal 335S
146 Clear Westmoreland with
    filigree 535R
147 Clear Pear lamp. 335R
148 Clear and frosted combination . . . 275
    All clear glass 235
149 Unassembled Figure 150
150 Bullseye chamber lamp with
    shade 425VR
151 Clear and frosted 265
152 Goofus paint on clear glass 135
    Clear, no paint 100
153 Milk glass, goofus paint 125
    Clear 110

154 Clear 110
    Milk glass 130
155 Clear 105
156 Milk glass 130
    Clear 105
157 Milk glass 165
    Clear 135
158 Milk glass 275S
159 Milk glass 265S
160 Milk glass 265
161 Milk glass 265
162 Milk glass 265
163 Milk glass Mug lamp 295S
164 Clear Tumbler lamp 225S
165 Clear Gothic Arch, handled 235S
166 Clear Grecian Key 75
167 Clear Grecian Key 115
    Pink, blue, green 175
168 Grecian Key, clear. 110
169 Grecian Key, milk glass 165S
    Grecian Key, clear. 115S
170 Rose-like lamp. 175S
171 Clear, painted embossed lilies 125
172 Milk glass 145
    Clear 125
173 Milk glass 125
    Clear 95
    Green glass 140S
174 Milk glass swirl 250S
175 Milk glass 145
    Clear 95
    Green glass 150S
176 Milk glass 300R
177 Custard, blue pink milk glass 275
    White milk glass 250
178 Blue, pink with filigree 435R
179 Blue milk glass 180S
    Blue, amber glass 195S
    Clear glass. 95
180 Milk glass 235S
    Blue, green milk glas 260S
181 Blue milk glass, pink opaline 325R
182 White bristol 220S
183 Milk glass 175
184 Milk glass (Fostoria, ca. 1898) . . . 250
185 Embossed milk glass 285S
186 Milk glass, painted satin finish . . . 245S
187 Milk glass, green glass. 145
188 Milk glass, Torquay pattern. 250S
189 Milk glass, Torquay pattern. 240
190 Block and Dot, milk glass 125
    Block and Dot, clear glass 120S
191 Block and Dot, milk glass 125
    Block and Dot, clear glass 120S
192"Mission" lamp, milk glass 75

"Mission" lamp, clear glass 85
193"Apple Blossom," milk glass 290
194"Apple Blossom," milk glass 280
195Northwood Glass Co., ca. 1896,
milk glass "Apple Blossom"
lamp......................... 395S
196Milk glass 145
Blue, green milk glass 180
197"Kenova Night Lamp," milk
glass 250S
198Embossed milk glass 190
199Embossed milk glass 215
Clear glass..................... 175
200Embossed milk glass 275
201Embossed milk glass 300S
202"Centennial Lamp" 300S
Painted flowers 310S
203Note: The Plume lamp has been
reproduced by L.G. Wright Company
in recent years in both cased and
uncased satin glass in various colors.
Know your glass and know your dealer.
203Milk glass (OLD) 250
204Clear 110
Milk glass 165
205Milk glass 175
Clear 120
206"Sunflower," embossed milk
glass 335S
207Embossed milk glass 335S
208Embossed milk glass 335S
209Embossed milk glass 335
210Embossed milk glass 225
211Embossed milk glass 225
212Pink, blue, green, white milk
glass 365S
213Embossed milk glass 350
Embossed red satin 360
214Embossed milk glass 210
215Custard, pink, yellow, blue milk
glass 375S
White milk glass 335S
216Custard, pink, yellow, blue milk
glass 385S
White milk glass 335S
217Brady's Night Lamp, green, pink, blue
milk glass 400S
Above colors, satin finish 425S
White milk glass 335S
218Milk glass 350R
Blue satin 375R
219Milk glass 150
Transparent colored glass........ 175S
220Milk glass 285S
Orange satin glass 385R

221Blue milk glass 450R
Painted milk glass 325S
222Milk glass, painted yellow or
butterscotch 350R
223White, green milk glass 265S
224Embossed milk glass 300
225Embossed milk glass 300
226Embossed milk glass 300
227Jr. size milk glass 335S
228Note: Again, let the buyer beware! This,
too, has been reproduced in cobalt,
vaseline, clear and a light marigold. If
you know your glass, you won't be
easily fooled by this one. Always
remember that the old fleur de lis lamps
are quite light in weight and that there is
a difference in base size (2-9/16" repro
height, 3" on old). The new has a hornet
size collar instead of nutmeg.
228Milk glass fleur de lis 275S
Clear glass fleur de lis 165S
229Milk glass, embossed 300
Milk glass green, blue 350
Green satin finish.............. 475S
230Milk glass 265
Blue milk glass 345S
231Note: This lamp was reproduced by
L.G. Wright Glass Company in various
colors of satin glass, red, pink and green,
to name a few. Examples were displayed
in the company showroom at the Dallas
Merchandise Mart within the past 20
years at a cost of $12.95. Caveat
Emptor!
231Milk glass, blue, pink shadings ... 300
Blue, green, red, pink satin....... 350
232Embossed milk glass 350S
233Blue, pink milk glass 360S
234Blue, green milk glass 330
White milk glass 275
235Blue milk glass 350S
236Milk glass 275
237Milk glass 300S
238Milk glass 325
239Embossed milk glass 325S
240Milk glass, painted flowers 275
Blue, green milk glass 350
241Milk glass, painted flowers 300
Blue, green milk glass 350
242Snail pattern milk glass 350S
Snail pattern frosted glass........ 425R
243Milk glass 275
244Milk glass 275
245Milk glass 325S
246"Erminie" night lamp 525R

247 Embossed milk glass 350S

248 Hanging lamp with prisms 2500R

249 Hanging lamp 1500R

250 "Diana" milk glass lamp 400R

251 Hanging lamp 1150VR

252 Hanging lamp 2250VR

253 Hanging reflector lamp 625VR

254 Clear 150S

    Painted clear 175S

255 White milk glass 300

    Custard, blue milk glass, greenish

    vaseline 350

256 Milk glass with various colors 200

    Clear glass 150

257 Custard, blue, green, amethyst . . . 350

    White milk glass 300

258 Amethyst, blue, green glass 325

259 Frosted clear glass 225S

260 Cobalt, green, amethyst glass 325

    Blue milk glass 325

261 Blue, green, amethyst glass 375S

262 Custard 300

    Cobalt, light and dark green,

    amethyst 325

    Crystal 175S

263 Blue, pink milk glass, custard 400R

264 Textured milk glass 400R

265 Milk glass with green, yellow, or

    pink trim 300

    Blue Delft scenes 375R

    Painted floral decoration 350S

266 Embossed milk glass 350S

267 Embossed milk glass 350S

268 Embossed milk glass 350S

269 Saucer base milk glass 385S

270 Embossed milk glass 350R

271 Embossed milk glass 375S

272 Brown, red, blue decoration 350

    Amber, green glass 375S

273 Embossed milk glass 350

    Red, pink satin 400S

274 Green or reddish paint 325S

275 Eagle lamp, painted decoration . . . 400

276 Milk glass, brown paint 300

    Green milk glass, green glass 325

277 Milk glass basket lamp 250S

    Clear glass 275R

278 Milk glass 225

    Clear glass 175

279 Yellow, pink, ice blue cased 610S

    Blue, pink, yellow satin 625S

    Green iridescent 700VR

280 Pink milk glass, rough finish 430S

281 Shell lamp 275S

282 Blue, pink milk glass, custard 365S

    White milk glass 300S

283 Embossed milk glass 350S

284 Red satin 250

    Blue, green satin 345S

285 Red satin 475

    Pink, green satin 540S

286 Milk glass, yellow, blue, pink

    trim 325

    Clear, frosted or painted 50-75

    Yellow, pink cased 500

287 Overshot, apricot shading 575S

    Overshot, green or pink

    shading 540S

    Painted milk glass 385S

    Red satin 425S

288 Red satin 510S

    Orange satin 600R

289 Blue, green, pink milk glass 385S

290 Pink and white spatter glass 550R

291 Porcelain base, milk glass

    shaded 410S

292 Frosted "Spider Web" 425R

    Milk glass, painted 350

    Red satin 375S

293 Pink, blue, green satin, clear satin with

    painted flowers, orange

    iridescent 425S

    Note: Not to be confused with much

    later clear glass lamp. The above lamp is

    made in a 4—section mold, presumed to

    be Northwood, while the newer one is a

    2—mold lamp.

294 Honey, pink spatter glass 495S

295 Porcelain base, milk glass

    shading 395S

296 "Sylvan" milk glass 250

297 Custard, blue milk glass 335

    White milk glass 295

298 Honey, pink spatter, filigree 1200VR

299 Pea green, blue, custard, white

    satin 425S

300 Light green satin with flowers 450S

301 Milk glass with filigree 950R

302 Red satin 500S

303 Milk glass with painted flowers . . 485S

304 Milk glass, brass pedestal 485S

305 Pairpoint banquet lamp 850S

306 Three-tier banquet lamp 750S

307 Milk glass, "Bohemian

    Boudoir" 575R

308 Milk glass, yellow, pink

    decoration 325

309 Pan-American lamp 425S

310 Green, blue, white milk glass 350

311 Painted milk glass 350S

Blue, orange, dark pink 675R
392 White satin, blue milk glass...... 400S
393 White satin, painted decoration .. 325
394 Pink, yellow, blue satin 450
Pink, green, blue, yellow cased with crystal (green scarce)............ 475
395 Blue, deep rose satin glass....... 650R
396 Blue satin 475R
White milk glass 345
397 Red satin glass 475S
398 Red satin glass 475S
399 Red satin glass 475S
Orange, blue satin glass 575R
400 Highly reproduced by L.G. Wright Glass Company in red, amber, white, pink satin, glossy white milk glass and cranberry, be very cautious of this one. The heavier, thicker glass, as opposed to the thinner glass of the old, is the tip-off.
Red satin...................... 300
Green, blue, pink satin 375S
401 Red satin...................... 460S
402 Peacock blue satin glass 510S
403 Note: Here is another reproduction to be leery of. Once again, let the weight and thickness of glass guide you *but* understand that the old lamp was no light-weight. Judge this one also on collar and burner and make certain they have not been changed.
White opalescent, ruby thumb print.
OLD 400S
404 Pink, blue opaline 445S
405 Red satin 465S
406 White satin 425S
407 White opaline 475S
408 Blue, pink opaline 475S
409 Blue, pink opaline 485S
410 Pink, blue opaline 480S
411 Overshot, purple glass 535R
412 Cranberry Mary Gregory 800VR
413 Overshot 525R
414 Overshot, clear to green 525S
415 Frosted with embossed dots 475R
416 Frosted glass................... 410
417 Rainbow glass 625R
418 Clear glass, painted green........ 185S
419 Note: The Daisy and Button lamp has been reproduced in various colors of transparent glass and white milk glass. However, there is a variance in size and contour of the old and new. Novice collectors should seek expert guidance on this one.
White with rainbow luster....... 400R

420 Frosted glass, enamel decoration.................... 400S
421 Iridescent pink swirl 525R
422 White iridescent glass 475S
423 Red, honey embossed........... 450S
424 Brown iridescent 410S
425 Green iridescent, embossed 485S
426 Clear, painted blue glass......... 395S
427 Clear, painted.................. 410S
428 White overshot 550S
429 White overshot 525S
430 Clear, painted.................. 425S
431 Rubina Ivy crystal.............. 585S
Rubina Ivy frosted 625S
432 Twinkle, blue, amethyst, green, teal 325
433 Blue, cranberry Honeycomb 500S
434 Cranberry, amber thumb print ... 325
Note: A similar reproduction has been made that could put Figure 434 in jeopardy. It came in cranberry thumb print and opalescent coin-spot. The base is smaller, and the umbrella shade slopes right into the tripod without the inset flange common to the old lamp.
435 Green paneled swirl 135
436 Green paneled swirl 135
437 Cranberry glass 410S
438 Cranberry glass 410S
439 Amberina glass 525S
Green opalescent, 500.00, yellow opalescent vaseline glass........ 525R
Cranberry 375S
Milk glass 235
440 Amberina glass 550R
441 Cranberry glass 475S
442 Cranberry glass 440S
443 Cranberry, blue glass 475S
Pink to rose cased satin 800R
444 Cranberry glass 525S
445 Amber embossed glass 400
446 Blue, cranberry glass 425
447 Blue, enamel decoration......... 425S
448 Amber glass 410S
449 Green, blue, amber glass 275
Milk glass 300
450 Green glass 350
451 Amber glass 325
452 Green glass 200S
453 Amber, blue, green glass 275
454 Green glass 300S
455 Green, blue porcelain 285
456 Dark and light green glass 285S
457 Green glass 360
458 Blue glass, enameled flowers 425S

459 Cranberry glass 375
460 Cranberry glass 375
461 Cranberry glass applied feet...... 735VR
462 Cranberry glass 575S
463 Blue glass lighthouse 535VR
464 Blue glass 385
465 Cranberry glass (top cut off?) 325R
466 Green, cranberry glass 460S
467 Blue, green glass................ 175
    Clear glass..................... 150
468 Green swirled glass 310
469 Green, cranberry glass 385
470 Green, blue, cranberry glass...... 410
471 Blue, cranberry Spanish lace 685S
    Vaseline Spanish lace 725S
472 Blue, amber glass............... 400S
473 Blue Spanish lace with filigree .. 1500VR
474 Reddish purple Spanish lace 1800VR
475 Blue swirled glass 360S
    Clear swirled glass.............. 225S
476 Amber glass 500S
    Clear glass..................... 375S
477 Blue, amber glass............... 425S
    Crystal....................... 325S
478 Clear glass "Famous" 350R
    Green glass "Famous" 500R
479 Amber, blue glass 450R
480 Amber, sapphire, cobalt 465S
    Vaseline...................... 495S
    Crystal....................... 325S
481 Blue, amber 450VR
    Crystal....................... 335R
482 Note: Reproductions by L.G. Wright were made in Amberina, blue, green, and milk glass. Differences noted between old and new: the new shade is taller (2⅝" new, 2⅜" old); the font of the new lamp is more apple-shaped. It was not reproduced in clear glass, so you are safe on that one.
    Blue, amber glass............... 360
    Vaseline...................... 425R
    Clear 300
483 Dresden base, bristol shade 485R
484 Porcelain House lamp........... 485R
485 Bisque boy with cart 700VR
486 Jasper ware 600VR
487 Porcelain Chinaman 320S
488 Reclining Elephant 750S
489 Bisque Boy and Girl, pr 1200VR
490 Bisque Skeleton lamp 6500VR
491 Columbus lamp 4200VR
492 Reclining Camel 1600VR
493 Clear 1000VR
    green milk glass 1400VR

    Blue milk glass 2000VR
494 Bulldog, frosted glass 1500VR
    Bulldog, milk glass 1350VR
495 Bisque Owl................... 2750VR
496 Porcelain Cat 750R
497 Owl, milk glass, painted gray ... 1950S
    Owl, milk glass, painted green .. 1900S
498 Porcelain Turtle lamp........... 750VR
499 Blue, pink, green milk glass 2250S
    White milk glass 2100R
    Pink satin finish 2250R
    Clear glass.................... 2100VR
500 Brown pottery Pig 950R
501 Milk glass Owl head........... 275S
    Frosted Owl head 275S
502 Opalescent threaded glass 950R
503 Ribbed pink opalescent 925R
504 Chrome green Aventurine 800VR
505 Greenish glass, threaded
    with red...................... 875VR
506 Green opalescent hobnail........ 675VR
507 Opalescent thumb print finger lamp with original chimney .... 475S Warning: Be aware of the numerous chimneys from modern electric lamps that seem to be finding their way into the hands of collectors.
508 Clear Spanish lace.............. 725S
    Cranberry Spanish lace 1150R
509 Clear and opalescent swirl....... 775R
    Blue, pink opalescent swirl 975R
510 White opalescent 725S
    Blue, pink, red opalescent 1200S
511 Cranberry—opalescent stripes.... 750R
512 Clear—opalescent swirl 400S
    Vaseline, blue—opalescent 525S
    Amber glass 490S
513 Cranberry, blue—opalescent 875S
    Clear—opalescent 575S
514 Yellow opalescent swirl 900R
    Red swirl..................... 800R
515 Opalescent—pink and clear 985R
516 Red glass—opalescent stripes 750R
517 Opalescent, applied blue feet..... 925S
518 Vaseline, opalescent thumb
    print 950VR
519 Cranberry, opalescent stripes..... 800R
520 Vaseline, opalescent 950R
521 Pale blue opalescent 800R
522 Pale pink opalescent 2750VR
523 Blue opalescent 1075S
524 Blue opalescent 1200R
525 Milk glass, amber trim 900R
526 Cranberry glass 975S
527 Diamond pattern cranberry 1050R

528 Candy-stripe cased glass 1200R	**569**Chartreuse cased glass 1050S
529 Candy-stripe case glass 1200R	**570**White to green satin 1200S
530 Pink cased, ribbed swirl 1150R	Pink to white satin 1200S
531 White, yellow, blue cut velvet. . . 1425R	**571**Signed Crown Milano 3275VR
532 White satin, ribbed swirl 1300R	**572**Yellow satin glass 1450S
533 Yellow, blue satin cut velvet 1650VR	**573**Pink to white satin, shade top cut off
534 Blue cut velvet 1525VR	(see No. 568) 525
535 Diamond pattern cranberry 950S	**574**Fireglow, melon base 2600VR
536 Cranberry, applied feet 975S	**575**Orange satin glass 1400VR
Amberina, applied feet 1250R	**576**Chartreuse Verre Moire 3250VR
537 Sterling, cranberry 1000VR	**577**Shaded rose Verre Moire 2800VR
538 Amberina glass 1200R	**578**Rose Verre Moire 2500VR
Cranberry 975R	**579**Red satin glass 1800VR
Pink, pinkish-green opalescent . . 1150S	**580**White and clear Verre Moire . . . 2100R
539 Pink ribbed swirl 1150R	**581**Blue and white Verre Moire 2000R
Apricot satin ribbed swirl 1400VR	**582**Red and beige Verre Moire 2450R
540 Cranberry to clear swirl 900R	**583**Green satin, silver berries 1200R
541 Raspberry satin 1300R	**584**Green glass 1150R
Blue satin 1200S	**585**Frosted glass, enameled
Clear satin 975S	decoration 1300R
542 Yellow, blue over white cased . . 1100S	**586**Tiffany, greenish-gold 2150R
Tomato Bisque cased 1125S	**587**Tiffany, greenish-gold
543 Amber and honey swirl 1250S	unassembled 2150R
544 Butterscotch ribbed swirl 1450VR	**588**Ribbed swirl satin MOP 2000VR
545 Cobalt ribbed swirl 1100S	**589**Ribbed swirl satin MOP 1450R
546 Cranberry ribbed swirl 1000S	**590**Green satin, brass pedestal 900R
547 End of Day cased glass 1225R	**591**Chartreuse satin MOP 1500VR
Yellow cased glass 1100R	**592**Pink satin MOP 1550VR
Overshot and crackle glass 1400R	**593**Rainbow satin MOP 2500VR
Dark cranberry 975R	**594**Rose satin MOP 1675R
Blue milk glass 900R	**595**Apricot satin MOP 1700R
548 End of Day glass 1100S	**596**Raspberry MOP 2700VR
549 End of Day Glass 1150S	**597**Blue, pink embossed MOP 1550R
550 Millefiori satin glass 1350VR	**598**White satin raindrop MOP 1600R
551 End of Day glass 1225R	**599**Left: Raspberry MOP 1825VR
552 Milk glass, applied cherries 875VR	Right: Rose, blue, green 1850VR
553 Cut overlay 3200VR	**600**Blue satin MOP 1675R
554 Gold-washed base, satin shade . . . 850VR	**601**Pink, green, blue, yellow 1450R
555 White glossy glass 900R	White satin MOP 1400R
Butterscotch with pink, red 950R	**602**Yellow satin MOP 1750R
Pink, butterscotch satin 975R	**603**Yellow satin MOP 1725R
556 Sterling base, embossed shade . . 1500VR	**604**Royal Worcester 1000VR
557 Yellow to white, in holder 1275R	**605**Baccarat Amberina 1000S
558 Gold-plated Rooster 1600VR	**606**Pink Baccarat 1500VR
559 Brass banquet lamp 850R	**607**Burmese 4000VR
560 Peg saucer-base 925VR	**608**Burmese, signed Webb 4000VR
561 Brass base, pottery font 850R	**609**Silver base, Burmese shade 2000VR
562 Green glass-rose opaline 1200VR	**610**Burmese, signed Webb 4000VR
563 Rose satin glass 1175R	**611**Tri-color Cameo 5750VR
564 Satin glass, embossed shells 1325R	**612**Cinnamon-brown Cameo 5550VR
565 Apricot satin glass 1300R	Note: The following lamp bases are
566 Salmon cased glass 1800VR	being priced on an incomplete basis
567 Pink overshot 2400VR	according to quality and design. The
568 Embossed pink satin 1075S	general rule-of-thumb is 20% of
Chartreuse satin 1150S	completed lamp value for bases, 40&

for shades. These prices have been figured accordingly in most instances.

613 Cased glass finger lamp 175VR
614 Embossed milk glass 100VR
615 Porcelain, double handles 100VR
616 Porcelain, girl 125VR
617 White, cut to blue Cameo 800VR
618 Bisque Swan 475VR
619 Bisque Cat 175VR
620 Crown Milano 250VR
621 Blue milk glass 175S
622 Columbus, pink milk glass 450VR

623 Porcelain elephant 250VR
624 Ruby, green, amethyst, amber 125
625 Same
626 Clear Glow lamp 125
627 Same
628 Milk glass with painted designs... 150
   Ruby, green amethyst, blue, amber
   glass 175
629 Nailsea Verre Moire fairy lamp .. 500
630 Vapo-Cresolene, left: .... 40—60
   Vapo-Cresolene, right: 50—75

Fig. 1 Brass hanging float lamp with cranberry insert font. $225.00 VR *Feltner collection.*

Fig. 2 Float lamp with metal base and hanger; etched font clear glass. 4 ⅝ inches tall. $125.00 R *Feltner collection.*

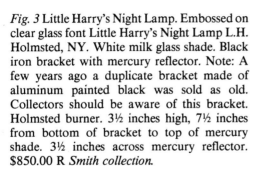

Fig. 3 Little Harry's Night Lamp. Embossed on clear glass font Little Harry's Night Lamp L.H. Holmsted, NY. White milk glass shade. Black iron bracket with mercury reflector. Note: A few years ago a duplicate bracket made of aluminum painted black was sold as old. Collectors should be aware of this bracket. Holmsted burner. 3½ inches high, 7½ inches from bottom of bracket to top of mercury shade. 3½ inches across mercury reflector. $850.00 R *Smith collection.*

Price Guide
for Miniature Lamps II

Introduction to Book II

Collectors will find that there is something for everyone in book II. Tastes differ the world around, and while one collector may revel in the beauty of art glass, another may lean in the opposite direction and take his or her pleasure in the simplistic or primitive. It is easy enough to determine our own preferences in lamps; it is quite another thing to establish the value of these treasures. And make no mistake, many are so skillfully executed that they can only be classified as such—and they must be valued accordingly.

Each and every lamp in this book has been duly considered as to scarcity, desirability and quality. We have agonized over many, painstakingly matching feature for feature with comparable lamps. Others were more readily evaluated. Our aim has not been to set prices, but rather to provide a guideline for you, the collector, to go by in establishing your own limitations. It is our fervent hope that dealers will not feel compelled to apply these prices because "they are in the book." Rather, we would hope that they would take pleasure in passing on their "finds" to collectors at a fair and reasonable profit.

We do not propose to offer an annual or bi-annual price guide and, therefore, expect these prices to stand for some time. A knowledgeable antique dealer explains that a reliable price guide never really becomes outdated. He maintains that the value of a lamp can be determined by knowing the current value of any other lamp in the guide, then, adjusting price according to price guide ratio between the two lamps, i.e., if lamp A is $100 and lamp B is $1000, lamp B should always be 10x more valuable than lamp A. Newly discovered lamps may be valued in a similar fashion by placing them in a category with the lamps in the guide. If used in this manner, a guide should be applicable for years if the appraiser or collector keeps abreast of current market prices on particular miniature lamps. We concur with his thoughts and hope that you will, too.

However, we want to emphasize again that all prices quoted in Miniature Lamps in book I and book II are only intended to serve as a "Guide" and not warranted as to accuracy. Prices, also, vary on miniature lamps in different parts of the country, and vary considerably due to the fast rise in inflation.

147 Brass "Gimbal" 140S
148 Brass pedestal without shade 85
149 Three-tier, brass & copper 50R
150 Painted tin pedestal 55
151 Brass pedestal, bristol shade 75
152 Brass pedestal, bristol shade 75
153 Copper peg with glass font 165R
154 Brass pedestal saucer 75S
155 Brass stem, cobalt font 135R
156 Brass stem, glass font 125S
157 Brass stem, glass font 125S
158 Removable font, Delft
    decoration 110S
159 Clear stem, frosted font 140R
160 Clear stem, frosted font 135S
161 Atterbury "Prism" 120R
162 Clear stem 65
163 Clear stem 65
164 Embossed clear stem 110S
165 Embossed clear stem 110S
166 Embossed clear stem 110S
167 Clear Icicle pattern 110S
168 Embossed clear stem lamp 115R
169 Embossed clear stem lamp 110S
170 Embossed clear stem lamp 115S
171 Clear pedestal lamp 80
172 Clear pedestal lamp 85
173 Clear beehive font 75S
174 Clear stem, embossed base 75S
175 Clear stem 65
176 Clear stem 65
177 Clear stem 60
178 Clear stem 65
    Blue glass 100
179 Clear swirl, dated glass collar 65S
180 Frosted Bulls-eye 80
181 Blue stem with embossed font 120S
182 Clear hobnail perfume 15
183 Clear swirl perfume 15
184 Swirl with reflector 25
    Swirl without reflector 15
185 Both left and right 10
186 Vapo—Cresolene 20
187"Holophane" 35S
188"Little Puck" 25R
189 Milk glass, ribbed shade 35S
190 Satin or clear perfume 15
191 Dark amber "Mulga" 15
192 Cobalt Danish finger lamp 125S
193 Cobalt double handle 145S
194 Cranberry pedestal 100R
195 Green glass with shade 125
    Green glass without shade 75
196 Dark amber 125
197 Roman Key with shade 125S

198 Ruby pedestal with shade 135S
199 Embossed trademark finger 125S
200 Embossed trademark, blue, no
    shade 85S
201 Brass finger with shade 75
202 Brass finger 40
203 Green glass, with shade, snuffer . . . 125
204 Blue, camphor shade 135
205 Cranberry, diamond pattern 250R
206 Clear embossed finger 95
207 Clear embossed finger 75
208 Pottery finger lamp 275VR
209 Clear finger with shade holder . . . 125S
210 Columbian Exposition 125R
211 Brass pedestal, clear shade 110S
212 Green embossed base, clear
    shade 250R
213 Opalescent vaseline 250VR
214 Green glass, embossed beading . . . 250S
215 Cobalt glass 275
216 Blown glass 150S
217 Amber glass, painted
    decoration 275S
218 Green Twinkle, painted
    decoration 375R
219 Green glass, enamel decoration . . . 150
220 Blue glass, embossed ribbed
    shade 150S
221 Blue glass, embossed beading 225S
222 Clear embossed glass 185R
223"Duchess" lamp, Cambridge 125S
224"Countess" lamp, Cambridge 125S
225 Bead & Panel, Fostoria, clear 125S
    Bead & Panel, cobalt, green 150R
226 Orange-amber finger lamp 225R
227 Turquoise with silver transfer 265R
228 Clear glass McKee & Brothers . . . 325R
    Blue, amber McKee &
    Brothers 410R
229 Cobalt embossed base 225R
230 Cranberry embossed ribbed 435VR
231 Blue-green, amber 375S
232 Green glass 250S
233 Cranberry swirl 375S
234 Clear melon-ribbed swirl, Duncan's
    Narrow Swirl 335S
235 Clear embossed thumb print,
    ribbed 385VR
236 Clear and frosted 275
    Clear 225
    Blue milk glass 375R
    Blue satin 425VR
237 Clear embossed swirl 425VR
238 Log Cabin, amber, blue, milk
    glass 625S

Log Cabin, clear .... 350S, ... white opaline 695S

Log Cabin, blue opaline 775R

239 Milk glass, painted flowers 125R

240 Novelty, seashells 75

241 Milk glass, rose petals 135S

242 Goofus, embossed roses, clear 135

Goofus, embossed roses milk glass......................150S

243 Wild Rose, clear 135S

244 Olive green porcelain 300S

245 Clear, painted ground 185S

246 Milk glass, embossed ribbed swirl 395R

247 "Dixie," by Fostoria 345R

248 Milk glass, embossed design, shade is original 285R

249 Blue, green, pink milk glass 400S

White milk glass 325S

250 Embossed milk glass 275S

251 Milk glass pedestal 165S

252 Harrison commemorative 425VR

253 Green, blue, white milk glass 300S

254 Yellow cased (Book I, No. 547) if perfect 1175R

255 White luster with prisms 550VR

256 "Primrose," white milk glass 400R

"Primrose," blue, green milk glass......................500R

257 "Wild Iris," milk glass 350

258 Embossed milk glass 325S

259 Embossed milk glass 135

260 Milk glass, painted decoration 300S

261 Light green satin 625R

262 Milk glass, painted decoration 325

263 Milk glass, painted ground 325S

264 Milk glass, painted ground 275

265 Milk glass, painted pansies 175

266 Milk glass, painted decoration 225

267 Dresden milk glass 525S

268 Milk glass, applied handle 235S

269 Milk glass, applied handle 275R

270 Melon ribbed white milk glass ...135

Melon ribbed blue, pink milk glass 175

271 Milk glass bear figural 265VR

272 Milk glass 135R

273 Figurine with milk glass font.....500VR

274 Milk glass shoe, no handle.......700VR

275 Brass pedestal 135R

276 Brass pedestal lamp............. 75S

277 Brass saucer hand lamp 175R

278 Brass pedestal lamp.............. 95S

279 Pewter embossed pedestal base... 265VR

280 Brass Jr. Rochester base 200S

281 Nickel-plated Bradley & Hub 200R

282 Brass jeweled lamp 150S

283 Brass saucer pedestal........... 110S

284 Brass pedestal with cased shade .. 150S

285 Brass pedestal jeweled 145S

286 Brass pedestal jeweled 145S

287 Brass pedestal jeweled 145S

288 Brass pedestal jeweled 300S

289 Brass pedestal with handle, wrong shade 85

290 Brass pedestal, bristol font 250R

291 Nickel-plated "Lampe—Pigeon", shade questioned.................... 135S

292 Brass saucer stem lamp......... 125S

293 Lamp post style fluid lamp 185R

294 Brass stem, milk glass shade 125S

295 Student lamp mfg. adv. .... N/A

296 Single brass student lamp....... 850S

297 Single brass student lamp....... 900R

298 Single brass student lamp....... 750R

299 Single brass student lamp....... 850S

300 Single brass student lamp....... 325S

301 Double brass student lamp 475S

302 Double brass log student lamp ... 850R

303 Double brass student lamp 1335R

304 Double brass student lamp 1800VR

305 Double brass sleigh lamp........ 900VR

306 Brass single sleigh 700R

307 Brass Barrel bracket 700VR

308 Brass spice lamp 525R

309 "Grand Val's Perfect Time"...... 250VR

310 Weaver Time lamp............. 245VR

311 Illuminated Clock 1200VR

312 German alarm clock 1100VR

313 Brass tray lamp, shade questioned.................... 125S

314 Brass tray lamp 175S

315 Blacksmith's figural lamp........ 175S

316 Iron Barrel adv. lamp 475VR

317 Bisque barrel, monkey handle.... 250VR

318 Porcelain with monkey 225VR

319 Luster porcelain camel 450VR

320 Porcelain Spitz dog 750VR

321 "Lady Fox," porcelain 825VR

322 Brown glazed Pug 800VR

323 Green porcelain Dog's head 625VR

324 Porcelain Tiger's head w/wicker shade 800VR

325 Porcelain Ram's head 825VR

326 Pair Majolica chickens 675VR

327 Bisque Swan and Egg 695VR

328 Performing Elephant............ 825VR

329 Porcelain Elephant 900VR

330 Porcelain Elephant, shade not original 950VR

331 Bisque cherub, butterfly 375VR
332 Porcelain with cherubs 475VR
333 Dresden porcelain with cherubs . . 750R
334 Porcelain with cherubs heads 150R
335 Dresden base, prisms/shade 500VR
336 Jasperware Oriental figural 625VR
337 Pair porcelain, Boy, Girl 800VR
338 China figural, ball shade 475R
339 China figural, wicker shade 475R
340 China figural, wicker shade 475R
341 China figural, wicker shade 700VR
342 Bisque Girl with Cart, wicker
    shade 700VR
343 Bisque Lamb with cherubs 550VR
344 Bisque child in blanket 550VR
345 Bristol with painted angels 150R
346 Blue glass, Mary Gregory 825VR
347 Green glass, Mary Gregory
    base 165R
348 Blue glass, Mary Gregory base . . . 165R
349 Santa Claus, painted gun
    metal 4000VR
350 Portrait lamp 425S
351 Portrait lamp 425S
352 Porcelain, Frankfort, Germany . . . 485S
353 Porcelain, Delft 300S
354 Milk glass, Seagull decoration 350R
355 Porcelain embossed base 300R
356 Oriental decoration, milk glass . . . 475VR
357 Milk glass, painted decoration 325R
358 Painted milk glass 400R
359 Milk glass, painted decoration 425R
360 Milk glass, painted decoration 425R
361 Bristol, painted decoration 410R
362 Green opaline, painted
    decoration 475R
363 White opaline, painted
    decoration 425S
364 Bristol, blue painted decoration . . 400S
365 Painted milk glass 350S
366 Milk glass, painted decoration 345S
367 White bristol, painted
    decoration 410S
368 Milk glass, blue bands
    (captioned wrong—should
    be 369) 475S
369 Blue glass with overshot (captioned
    wrong—should be 368) 550VR
370 Lavender bristol 535VR
371 Cobalt pedestal 375S
372 Blue milk glass (mismatched) 285
373 Milk glass, base only 80R
374 Bracket with cranberry font 675R
375 Bracket with cranberry font 550R
376 Hanging store lamp (chimney probably

    not original) 650VR
377 Hanging store lamp 750VR
378 Hanging Hall lamp 600R
379 Hanging Hall lamp 650VR
380 Hanging Hall lamp 1250VR
381 Hanging Hall lamp (if old) 1250R
382 Hanging Hall lamp (if old) 1250R
383 Hanging Hall lamp (if
    original) 1500VR
384 Hanging Hall lamp (if old) 850R
385 Brass boudoir lamp 100
386 Brass boudoir lamp 100
387 White metal boudoir lamp 110
388 Brass wall lamp 175R
389 Mercury base, peg Glow, pair
    (captioned wrong-should be
    No. 391) 650VR
390 Pair blue glass peg lamps 225S
391 Embossed brass with handle peg
    (captioned wrong-should be
    No. 389) 250VR
392 Pair tin peg lamps 275VR
393 Brass saucer peg lamp 80S
394 Candle-stick with china saucer . . . 475VR
395 Pairpoint chamber (complete) . . . 1000VR
396 Lavender ribbed milk glass 400VR
397 Milk glass, beaded fringe (captioned
    wrong-should be No. 398) 425R
398 (Wrong caption-should be No.397)
    Identical to Fig. No. 571, Book I, which
    is signed Crown Milano and we are
    pricing this one accordingly 3200VR
399 Embossed satin, base only 80S
400 Cobalt glass 175S
401 Cobalt embossed glass 475VR
402 Bristol with accent bands 425R
403 Pink cased satin 625S
404 Jr. sized red satin 600S
405 Porcelain, Victoria-Carlsbad 485S
406 Milk glass with roses 210S
407 Milk glass, floral decoration 325S
408 Porcelain with brass base 120R
409 Cranberry threaded (base) 110R
410 Art Nouveau copper 475VR
411 Amber glass, pewter pedestal 435VR
412 Blue-green glass with shade 325R
413 Bohemian, red to clear 600VR
414 Amber glass, Bohemian shade
    (mismatched) 125S
415 Blue font, metal pedestal 95R
416 Brass pedestal, frosted shade 185S
417 Silverplated base, frosted shade . . . 625R
418 Delft handled base 95VR
419 Porcelain pedestal base 575R
420 Delft banquet lamp 700R

421	Three-tier banquet lamp	800S
422	Brass filigree banquet lamp	675R
423	Three-tier satin banquet lamp (mismatched)	575S
424	Pairpoint banquet lamp	875S
425	Silverplated pedestal	450R
426	Brass pedestal, metal font	700VR
427	Cobalt porcelain, brass base	130VR
428	Silver pedestal, burmese shade	1250VR
429	Silver base, peachblow shade	1275VR
430	Brass pedestal, MOP satin	1900VR
431	Wrought iron base, brass font	475VR
432	Brass plated pedestal	550VR
433	Cloisonne, marble base	1250VR
434	Brass pedestal, oriental font	675VR
435	Gold-washed metal and tin	725VR
436	Embossed silver base	700VR
437	Pewter pedestal	285R
438	Brass plated pedestal	700VR
439	Porcelain owl, natural colors	900VR
440	Porcelain owl base only	700R
441	White china owl base	725VR
442	Porcelain owl head	350VR
443	Frosted green owl base	625VR
444	Stein lamp, owl decoration	1500VR
445	Stein lamp, Rugby scenes	1000R
446	Stein lamp, Golf motif	400R
447	Stein lamp, Monk motif	1000R
448	Three-tier pedestal	275R
449	Square base, enameled decoration	1000VR
450	Milk glass, with cupids	575VR
451	Porcelain handled lamp	550VR
452	Iron pedestal, bristol font	400R
453	Pink satin embossed pedestal	800R
454	Embossed chartreuse cased satin	1125VR
455	Embossed satin, mismatched	465R
456	Embossed pink satin	1100R
457	Cased ribbed swirl	775R
458	Heavily embossed milk glass	475R
459	Raspberry embossed satin	1125VR
460	Bristol, painted decoration	350R
461	Yellow cut velvet	300S
462	Lavender cut velvet	300S
463	Green cut velvet	300S
464	Pink cased, mismatched	300
465	Clear, painted satin finish	475R
466	Yellow spatter glass	700VR
467	Vaseline opalescent	1300VR
468	Rose and white spatter (mismatched)	550R
469	Spatter glass, ribbed swirl	1300VR
470	Green frosted glass	400VR
471	Green log or tree stump	425R

472	Amber glass pedestal	300S
473	Cranberry pedestal	450R
474	Cranberry paneled	575R
475	Dark aqua, enamel decoration	550R
476	Blue glass, enamel decoration	450VR
477	Cranberry glass, enamel decoration	485R
478	Cranberry with opaline flowers	600R
479	Lavender painted glass, overshot	650VR
480	Iridescent green textured glass	525R
481	Clear glass, winter scenes	475R
482	Acid finish, embossed design (mismatched)	275S
483	Clear, painted satin finish	450S
484	Clear, brushed finish	485R
485	Amberina ribbed swirl	625R
486	Amber glass	375S
487	Amber glass, enamel decoration	185VR
488	Amber glass, applied handle	85S
489	Cranberry embossed ribbed swirl	135S
490	Cranberry shading to clear	150VR
491	Blue glass, harlequin design	95R
492	Amberina quilted glass	935VR
493	Amberina, applied feet	1100VR
494	Shaded green glass	675S
495	Shaded green glass, applied feet	750S
496	Cobalt glass, enamel decoration	450S
497	Amber glass Nellie Bly	300S
498	Teal with crystal stem	350R
499	Cranberry, diamond-quilted	575VR
500	Cranberry opalescent	800VR
501	Vaseline opalescent	400VR
502	Opalescent bristol	485VR
503	Cranberry opalescent swirl	425VR
504	Opalescent, applied handle	700VR
505	Cranberry opalescent swirl	700VR
506	Cranberry opalescent stripes	700VR
507	Amber-honey swirl, mismatched	500VR
508	Opalescent with clear "eyes"	875VR
509	Shaded pink iridescent	700VR
510	Opalescent vaseline swirl	725VR
511	Opalescent paneled	700VR
512	Vasa Murrhina glass	750VR
513	Blue shaded glass	850VR
514	Cranberry embossed ribbed swirl	975VR
515	Vasa Murrhina base, amber shade (mismatched)	345VR
516	Orange cased glass	650S
517	Chartreuse satin glass	1100R
518	Parian, embossed design	1075VR
519	Amber with crackle overlay	1925VR

520Cranberry embossed diamond
   pattern 975R
521Amber, cranberry honeycomb . . . 800R
522Basket-weave base, MOP shade . . 550VR
523Pink glass, silver filigree 2200VR
524Blue satin MOP, applied feet . . . 1950VR
525Blue satin, enameled
   decoration 1800VR
526Burmese color satin glass 1650VR
527Satin Fireglow 2500VR
528Fireglow satin 2500VR
529Blue satin with birds 1500VR
530Satin glass, possible Webb 1500VR
531Thomas Webb burmese glass . . . 2750VR
532MOP satin with coralene 4650VR
533Rose MOP satin 2500VR
534Yellow MOP satin 2500VR

535Blue frosted overshot 1000VR
536Pink satin MOP 2250VR
537Vaseline overshot 1500VR
538Pink opalescent threaded 1650VR
539Pink opalescent threaded 1650VR
540Opalescent ribbed swirl 2650VR
541Raspberry Cameo 5550VR
542Pink and white Verre Moire 4000VR
543Wrought iron with cased fonts . . 1350R
544Cranberry, enamel decoration 600R
545Goofus stem 165
546Cranberry, enamel decoration 675VR
547Rainbow cut glass 4500VR
548Spatter glass, applied feet 1450R
549Pink shaded MOP satin 2400R
550Cased End-of-Day glass 1350VR

Fig. 4 Candle stick peg lamp with very ornate silver base of a coiled snake. Mouth of snake holds candle stick base while end of tail is curled to form finger hold. Small circular opening for matches at side of snake. White milk glass shade. Twilight shade holder burner. 12 inches high. $350.00 VR *Hulsebus collection.*

Fig. 5 Left: Tiny metal bracket lamp with brass reflector, embossed decorative detail. Foreign burner. 3¾ inches to top of hanger. $135.00 VR. Right: Copper base with brass reflector bracket lamp. Foreign burner. 3¾ inches to top of hanger. $75.00 S *Feltner collection.*

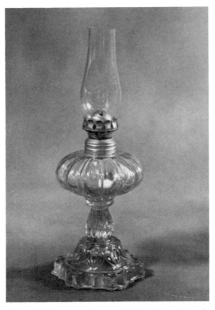

Fig. 6 Clear embossed ribbed pedestal base with lobed onion font, possibly Atterbury. Acorn burner. 5¼ inches to top of collar. $225.00 R *Feltner collection.*

Fig. 8 Silver-plated pedestal base, brick-colored painted satin font with blossoms and green leaves, amberina chimney. P & A Nutmeg burner. 4¼ inches to top of collar. $175.00 VR *Feltner collection.*

Fig. 7 Amber stem lamp, four panels separated by bands of horizontal ribbing, base has scalloped outer edge. Nutmeg burner. 5 inches to top of collar. $175.00 R *Feltner collection.*

Fig. 9 Regal Fancy Panel (proper name) made by Riverside Glass Company of Wellsburg, W. Va. Nutmeg burner. 5½ inches to top of collar. $145.00 R *Feltner Collection.*

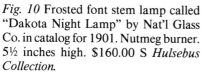

Fig. 10 Frosted font stem lamp called "Dakota Night Lamp" by Nat'l Glass Co. in catalog for 1901. Nutmeg burner. 5½ inches high. $160.00 S *Hulsebus Collection.*

Fig. 11 Clear glass embossed panel stem lamp. Acorn burner. 5½ inches high. $110.00 VR *Smith Collection.*

Fig. 12 Little Crown (proper name) lamp, cast iron embossed pedestal with clear ridged font. Circa 1877. Foreign burner. 3¾ inches to top of collar. $325.00 VR *Feltner collection.*

Fig. 14 Tiny Dresden-type porcelain square base lamp, pink trim, painted flowers in each panel. Foreign burner. 2⅜ inches to top of collar. $100.00 R *Feltner collection.*

Fig. 13 Very tiny Dresden-type lamp, fired on painted butterflies in brown and gold decorations on font. Applied flowers in various colors on pedestal base. Clear glass chimney. Burner similar to Fig. 402 in book II. Night lamp embossed on burner. 5½ inches to top of chimney. $350.00 VR *Smith collection.*

Fig. 15 Blue glass with tin reflector, embossed with quarter-moon face and "moon lamp," 5½ inches to top of reflector. $145.00 S *Feltner collection.*

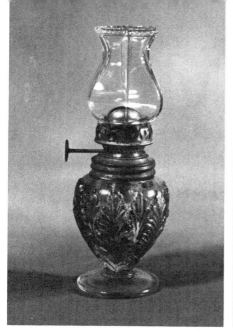

Fig. 16 One of a pair of goofus salt-shaker type lamps with 6-paneled shades beaded around the top edge. Acorn burner. 6 inches to top of shade. $95.00 S *Feltner collection.*

Fig. 18 Milk glass base, clear font, tiny bristol ovate shade. Olmsted type burner. 3¼ inches to top of collar. $275.00 VR *Feltner collection.*

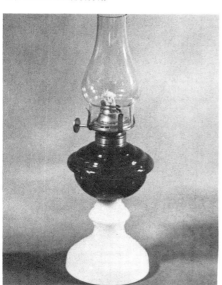

Fig. 17 White bristol pedestal base, sapphire blue font. Four prong burner size of Hornet. 5½ inches to top of collar. $250.00 VR *Feltner collection.*

Fig. 19 Left: Soft blue-green opaque glass with milk glass shade, painted white flowers in center of base. Dated collar. Olmsted burner. 2 inches to top of collar. $250.00 S *Feltner collection.* Right: Same as in left picture only in black opaque.

Fig. 20 Left: White milk glass lamp with colorful fired on flowers in shades of orange, blue, pink, green leaves. Foreign burner. 6 inches high. Right: White bristol glass lamp with fired on decorations in red and gold. Olmsted type burner. 4 inches high. Note: 1907 catalog of Burley & Tyrell Co. Chicago shows a picture of a lamp similar "Japanese Decorated". Price left $425.00 S. Price right $175.00 S *Hulsebus collection.*

Fig. 21 Soft green opaline finger lamp, gold bands still faintly visible. Dated collar. Milk glass shade. Olmsted burner. 2¼ inches to top of collar. $250.00 S *Feltner collection.*

Fig. 22 Clear glass base embossed on front of font "Triumph" on back of font "Wilmot Mfg, Co" white bristol shade. Olmsted tip-up type burner. 4 inches high. Right lamp disassembled. $150.00 VR *Lennox collection.*

Fig. 23 Brass finger saucer lamp with fancy embossed font; squatty beaded top chimney. Hornet burner. 1½ inches to top of collar. $95.00 S *Feltner collection.*

Fig. 25 Cramberry harlequin pattern finger lamp. Hornet burner. 3½ inches high. $175.00 R *Hulsebus collection.*

Fig. 24 Queens Necklace (proper name) pattern glass design made by Bellaire Glass Co. May or may not have had a matching shade. Acorn burner. 3½ inches to top of collar. $150.00 S *Feltner collection.*

Fig. 26 Pale lavender shading to clear paneled finger lamp with applied clear glass shell feet and handle. May or may not have had a matching shade. Foreign burner. 4 inches high. $375.00 R *Hulsebus collection.*

Fig. 27 Turquoise cased finger lamp with 3 clear glass applied feet and reeded handle. Hand painted flowers in orange and white. May or may not have had a matching shade. Foreign burner. 4 inches high. $475.00 R *Hulsebus collection.*

Fig. 28 Camphor glass base and chimney to match with clear stars. May or may not be old. Acorn burner. 6 inches high. $150.00 S *Hulsebus collection.*

Fig. 29 Bohemian type lamp, red cut to clear design on both base and chimney identical. Acorn burner. 7½ inches high. $300.00 S *Hulsebus collection.*

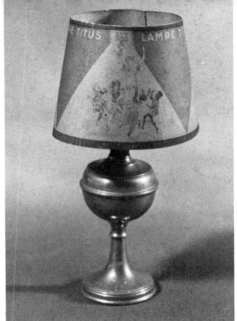

Fig. 30 Heavy clear glass base with ball shade; remnants of unfired painted flowers; reverse embossed design in foot. 7⅛ inches to top of shade. $95.00 S *Feltner collection.*

Fig. 32 Pewter pedestal lamp with original shade. French marked "Lampe Titus." Foreign burner 5½ inches to top of shade. $125.00 S *Feltner collection.*

Fig. 31 Cramberry glass, faintly swirl-ribbed in base and shade. Not very old, becoming very collectible. Similar to Fig. 503 in book II. Nutmeg burner. 8¾ inches high. $275.00 S *Nesses collection.*

Fig. 33 Brass pedestal lamp with heavily embossed font, green milk glass shade like Fig. 101 in book II. Nutmeg burner. 7¾ inches to top of shade. $150.00 R *Feltner collection.*

Fig. 34 White porcelain base with cobalt embossed wreaths and garlands. Bristol globe-chimney shade. Hornet-type burner. 7⅛ inches to top of shade. $165.00 R *Feltner collection.*

Fig. 36 Embossed ribbed pattern blue glass applied handle. Foreign burner. 6¾ inches high. $475.00 VR *Smith collection.*

Fig. 35 Blue glass slightly paneled, applied handle. Foreign burner. 6½ inches high. $250.00 S *Smith collection.*

Fig. 37 Unusual silver-plated finger lamp with engraved floral-leaf design; three cloven-hoof feet. Crystal ball shade is not original. Paris burner. 4 inches to top of collar. $500.00 VR *Feltner collection.*

Fig. 38 Amber glass embossed design lamp. Olmsted-type burner. 5½ inches high. $375.00 VR *Smith collection.*

Fig. 40 Blue glass Honeycomb pattern, applied crystal feet. Base differs from Fig. 433 in book I. Upturned lightly flared-out shade. Acorn burner. 6½ inches high. $850.00 R *Smith collection.*

Fig. 39 Blue glass lamp in Honeycomb pattern. Base differs from Fig. 433 in book I in size and design. Upturned lightly flared out shade. Acorn burner. 6½ inches high. $650.00 S *Hulsebus collection.*

Fig. 41 Blue opalescent lamp with faintly wide ribs. Clear applied shell feet. Shade like Fig. 521 in book I. Foreign burner. 7½ inches high. $800.00 *Lennox collection.*

Fig. 42 Amber glass, embossed pattern, called "VIVIAN" night lamp in Thuro book I, on oil lamps. Acorn burner. 8 inches high. $475.00 VR *Smith collection.*

Fig. 43 Emerald green, faintly paneled lamp. Foreign burner. 8 inches to top of shade. $375.00 S *Feltner collection.*

Fig. 44 Transparent blue ribbed swirl lamp. Base has four sides, shade has six sides. Foreign burner. 7¾ inches high. $850.00 R *Lennox collection.*

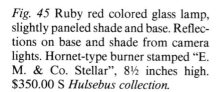

Fig. 45 Ruby red colored glass lamp, slightly paneled shade and base. Reflections on base and shade from camera lights. Hornet-type burner stamped "E. M. & Co. Stellar", 8½ inches high. $350.00 S *Hulsebus collection.*

Fig. 46 Pewter type metal lamp. Embossed floral, leaf and vine design. Acid etched ball shade marked "St Louis." Foreign burner. 12¼ inches high. $375.00 R *Lennox collection.*

Fig. 47 Blue glass pedestal base, clear font. Blue ball shade not original. Looks French, but American acorn burner fits. Foreign burner. 6¼ inches to top of collar. $200.00 S *Feltner collection.*

Fig. 48 Brass and porcelain pedestal lamp with acid etched ball shade. Font is white opaline and a portion of stem is pale pink porcelain with tiny white and blue flowers, green leaves. Foreign burner. 10 inches high. $450.00 S *Hulsebus collection.*

Fig. 49 Colorful Cloisonne lamp with brass footed stand. Frosted ball shade with gold decorations. Foreign burner. 9 ½ inches high. $975.00 VR *Lennox collection.*

Fig. 50 Fancy metal foot pedestal base, milk glass fired on paint; portraits of foreign women on shade and font. Foreign burner. 12½ inches to top of shade. $575.00 VR *Feltner collection.*

Fig. 51 Blue mottled porcelain handled base, lavender and orange pansy flowers, green leaves outlined with white dots on base and shade. Foreign burner. 9½ inches high. $475.00 R *Hulsebus collection.*

Fig. 52 Creamy porcelain square base, heavily embellished with applied porcelain flowers. Milk glass painted rosebud shade, not original but old and complementary. "The Silber Light Company" burner. 3⅞ to top of collar. $225.00 VR *Feltner collection.*

Fig. 53 Pink fading to white milk glass lamp, decorated with gold butterfly and white flowers. Ruffled upturned shade, clear to opalescent applied shell feet. Foreign burner. 10¾ inches high. $875.00 VR *Lennox collection.*

Fig. 54 Fired on painted milk glass lamp, background light blue flowers pink with aqua leaves. Foreign burner. 9¼ inches high. $350.00 S *Lennox collection.*

Fig. 55 Majolica petal base in shades of pink and yellow, opalescent petal-type shade in pink shading to very pale pink. Sparr-Brenner burner. 9¾ inches to top of shade. $750.00 R *Feltner collection.*

Fig. 56 Peach bristol glass lamp with large painted pansy flowers in lavender, green leaves. Foreign burner. 9 inches high. $350.00 S *Hulsebus collection.*

Fig. 57 Raspberry Swirl milk glass lamp, medallion design on base similar to Fig. 547 in book I. White bristol glass applied shell feet, center of dimple also white, umbrella type shade. This combination has been seen in satin as well as cased glass, also in blue and yellow. It can be assumed correct. Nutmeg burner. 8¼ inches high. $900.00 VR *Hulsebus collection.*

Fig. 58 Blue milk glass lamp with swirled ribbed square base and ball shade. Gold paint between ribs worn. Foreign burner. 9½ inches high. $875.00 R *Hulsebus collection.*

Fig. 59 Pink opaline glass lamp with spatter decorations in shades of bright red, brown and orange. Foreign burner. 7¼ inches high. $525.00 R *Hulsebus collection.*

Fig. 60 Aqua bristol glass lamp with fired on painted flowers in orange and white, leaves green and gray. Foreign burner. 8 inches high. $425.00 R *Hulsebus collection.*

Fig. 61 Fancy footed Dresden-type square porcelain base. Milk glass ball shade. Foreign burner. 11¾ inches to top of shade. $485.00 S *Feltner collection.*

Fig. 62 Thinly satinized green and orange paint over clear glass. Green, red and yellow fired on decorations. Base dimpled on 4 sides. Sparr Brenner burner. 9 inches high. $450.00 R *Hulsebus collection.*

Fig. 63 Blue bristol glass lamp with red strawberries and gold leaves. Small white painted dots around center of base and top rim of shade. Foreign burner. 9 inches high. $375.00 S *Hulsebus collection.*

Fig. 64 White milk glass lamp with rose and white floral decorations. Foreign burner. 10½ inches high. $225.00 S *Lennox collection.*

Fig. 65 White bristol-type glass lamp, old fashion Gibson girl dressed in bloomers and hat standing along side of bicycle. Fired on paint in blue. Acorn burner. 9 inches high. $1000.00 VR *Smith collection.*

Fig. 66 White bristol-type glass lamp, fired on painted faintly blue around top and bottom of base. Windmill scene in darker blue. Prima-Rund Brenner burner. 10 inches high. $1200 VR *Smith collection.*

Fig. 67 Delft porcelain, fired on painted boat scenes in blue, darker blue decorations. On bottom of base 3. Sparr Brenner burner. 8¼ inches high. $375.00 R *Nesses collection.*

Fig. 68 Tan and dark brown begging Pug dog. Green ball shade not original. Foreign burner. 6¼ inches to top of collar. $950.00 VR *Feltner Collection.*

Fig. 69 White poodle sitting on pink base, blue collar, excellent detail from teech right on down to toenails, rampant gold lion on clambroth shade. Wick turner marked "Prince & Symons, Lion Lamp Works, London, Manufactured in Germany." 9 inches to top of collar. $1150.00 VR *Feltner collection.*

Fig. 70 White porcelain cat with blue bow, tail between legs. Amber shade not original. Foreign burner. 6⅛ inches to top of collar. $850.00 VR *Feltner collection.*

Fig. 71 Green basketweave type porcelain base with cat and dog looking out on opposite sides. Animal heads are white. Shade and burner are incorrect. Markings on bottom of base "PS..L 5701." $550.00 VR *Hulsebus collection.*

Fig. 72 Tiger previously shown in book II, Fig. 324. Original fixtures. Shade may not be original. Wick turner reads "Lion Lamp Works" and depicts rampant lion. Blue anchor mark on bottom. 3 inches to top of collar. $950.00 R *Feltner collection.*

Fig. 73 Porcelain Lion Head lamp in shades of brown. Bottom of base has blue Anchor markings. Foreign burner. 3½ inches high. $800.00 R *Hulsebus collection.*

Fig. 74 Walrus porcelain base, green shading to white. Green porcelain shade not original but complementary. $750.00 R *Feltner collection.*

Fig. 75 Ruffled white porcelain owl with applied porcelain flowers at feet, milk glass shade. Foreign burner. 6½ inches to top of collar. $950.00 R *Feltner collection.*

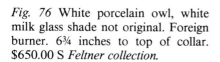

Fig. 76 White porcelain owl, white milk glass shade not original. Foreign burner. 6¾ inches to top of collar. $650.00 S *Feltner collection.*

Fig. 77 Owl lamp in sapphire blue shading to clear at bottom. Shade and base original. Also base made in rainbow cased glass. Sparr Brenner burner. 5¼ inches to top of collar. $1200.00 R *Feltner collection.*

Fig. 78 Green porcelain owl, white milk glass shade. French, foreign burner. 6¼ inches to top of collar. $650.00 S *Feltner collection.*

Fig. 79 Porcelain mushroom supported by three owls with applied ivy vines trailing over base. Frosted reverse-painted shade; shade may or may not be original. Foreign burner. 6¾ inches to top of collar. $750.00 R *Feltner collection.*

Fig. 80 Parian Owl, base is the shape of owls head, shade has owl sitting in half moon in 3 places, clouds around bottom of base, stars scattered throughout shade. Ridged top of shade and bottom of base. Nutmeg burner. 7½ inches high. $3200.00 VR *Hulsebus collection.*

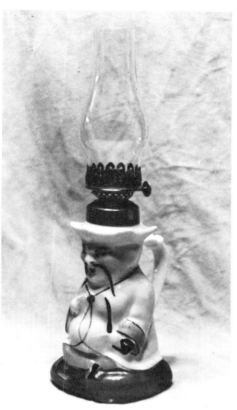

Fig. 81 Finger lamp depicting a "Chinaman" sitting on a brown cushion. Fired on paint on robe is blue, sleeve-bands in lavender. Foreign burner. 6 inches high. $625.00 VR *Hulsebus collection.*

Fig. 82 Porcelain base with Oriental seated with crossed legs. Robe painted green with gold detail. Etched Baccarat shade in green shading to almost clear. Foreign burner. 6½ inches to top of collar. $950.00 VR *Feltner collection.*

Fig. 83 Bisque girl sitting in a basket-canopy chair. Dress and shoes in shades of aqua. Aqua satin ball shade. Sparr Brenner burner. 9 inches high. $1000.00 VR *Hulsebus collection.*

Fig. 84 Porcelain base with applied Colonial man and woman at sides holding a garland of flowers between them, pink wash, touches of gold; milk glass shade with over-painted sprays of flowers. Foreign burner. 11¾ inches to top of shade. $475.00 R *Feltner collection.*

Fig. 85 Bisque girl and cart with pink and blue accents, pink bisque shade with three applied cherubs. Base like Fig. 342 in book II. Sparr Brenner burner. 9½ inches to top of shade. $180.00, shade very rare. *Feltner collection.*

Fig. 86 Bisque cherub supporting a beribboned and netted sheaf. Usual bristol shade used for many figurals. Kosmos-Brenner burner. 5 inches to top of collar. $575.00 R *Feltner collection.*

Fig. 87 Porcelain gondola with musician straddling the sternum of boat. White milk glass shade. Foreign burner. 3⅝ inches to top of collar. $200.00 S *Feltner collection.*

Fig. 88 Ornate porcelain pink and blue base with four bird-like gargoyle handles. Cased pink satin swirled shade. Foreign burner. 12½ inches to top of shade. $650.00 VR *Feltner collection.*

Fig. 89 Clear to light blue lightly paneled lamp with upturned ruffled shade. Foreign burner. 10 inches high. $750.00 VR *Hulsebus collection.*

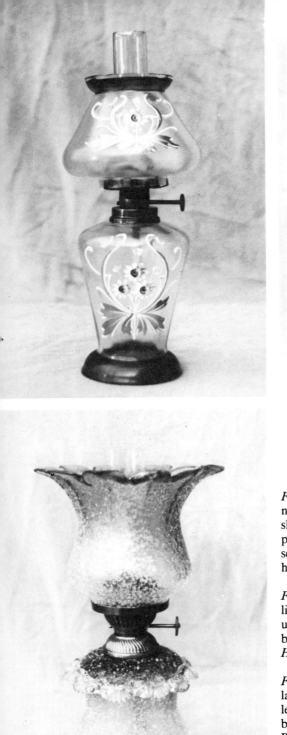

Fig. 90 Pearlized glass lamp with narrow light green bands at top of shade and bottom of base. Fired on paint of pink, white and gold floral and scrolls design. Foreign burner. 7½ inches high. $450.00 R *Hulsebus collection.*

Fig. 91 Cramberry overshot fading to light pink. Glass filigree on footed base, upturned petal edged shade. Foreign burner. 10¼ inches high. $650.00 VR *Hulsebus collection.*

Fig. 92 Clear textured opaque glass lamp with red and blue flowers, green leaves. Brass pedestal base. Foreign burner marked "B & L Patent Reform Brenner." 9½ inches. $750.00 VR *Hulsebus collection.*

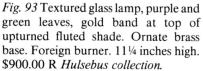

Fig. 93 Textured glass lamp, purple and green leaves, gold band at top of upturned fluted shade. Ornate brass base. Foreign burner. 11¼ inches high. $900.00 R *Hulsebus collection.*

Fig. 94 Light lavender textured opaque glass lamp with white metal base, decorated with orange leaves, white daisy type flowers. Foreign burner marked "P L." 13¼ inches high. $900.00 R *Hulsebus collection.*

Fig. 95 Opalescent vaseline lamp with reverse swirl similar to Fig. 544 in book I. Applied vaseline shell feet. Sparr Brenner burner. 8½ inches high. $1450.00 VR *Hulsebus collection.*

Fig. 96 Light blue opalescent ribbed lamp. Shade has narrow horizontal ribs, chimney and stem of lamp have narrow vertical ribs. Font has a wider vertical paneled rib. Sparr Brenner burner. 7¼ inches high. $1600.00 VR *Hulsebus collection.*

Fig. 97 Clear glass lamp with pink frosted band at bottom and top of base and shade. Decorations baked on enamel flowers in white and blue dots with red centers. Foreign burner. 7½ inches high. $425.00 S *Lennox collection.*

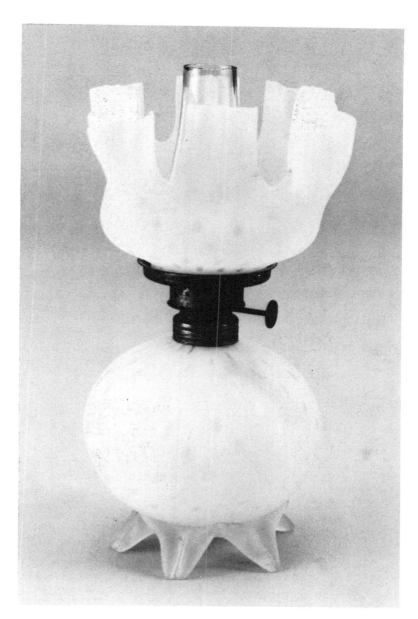

Fig. 98 White mother-of-pearl glass lamp with applied frosted feet. Note: The shade on this lamp is questionable. Several have examined the shade with a magnifying glass, the edges of the openings are rolled out as if they overlapped the mole. If the openings were broken and filed, the openings would be smooth and not overlapped. A dealer saw a lamp identical to this one in blue. The lamp is old; it would be interesting to know if someone else ever saw a shade with openings like in this one, similar to Fig. 602 in book I. Nutmeg burner. 8¾ inches high. If original, $1450.00 VR *Nesses collection.*

Fig. 99 Clear glass lamp covered with filigree in Spanish lace pattern. Note: Upturned shade is different from Fig. 474 in book I. Nutmeg burner. 8 ¼ inches high. $1300.00 VR *Smith collection.*

Fig. 100 Deep rose milk glass lamp with silver filigree on base and shade, same shape as Fig. 297 in book I. Nutmeg burner. 7½ inches high. $1400.00 VR *Hulsebus collection.*

Fig. 101 Ribbed swirled yellow satin glass lamp with applied frosted feet. Sparr-Brenner burner. 8 inches high. $1550.00 VR *Hulsebus collection.*

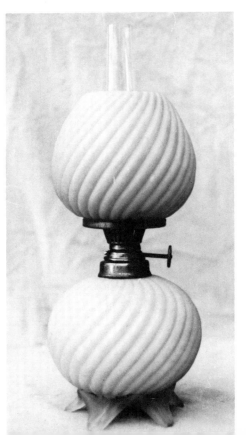

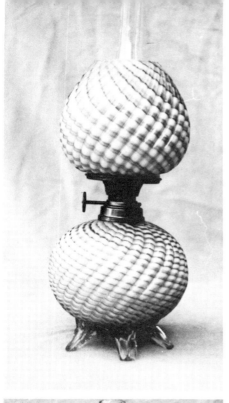

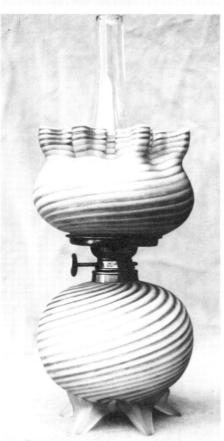

Fig. 102 Reverse swirl candy-stripe pink cased glass lamp with ball shade. Clear glass applied feet to base. Sparr Brenner burner. 8 inches high. $1350.00 VR *Hulsebus collection.*

Fig. 103 Green cased satin glass candy stripe lamp with applied frosted feet, upturned shade similar in shape to Fig. 527 in book I. Also comes in pink. "R. Ditmar Wien" marked burner. 7½ inches high. $1350.00 VR *Hulsebus collection.*

Fig. 104 Pink candy stripe lamp with clear applied feet, umbrella shade. Nutmeg burner. 8 inches high. $1350 VR *Hulsebus collection.*

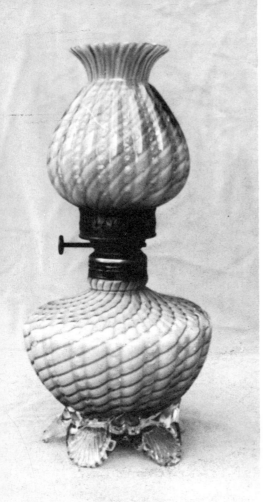

Fig. 105 Pink swirled beaded candy stripe lamp, clear applied feet. Similar to Fig. 367 in book I. Hornet burner. 9½ inches high. $1800.00 VR *Hulsebus collection.*

Fig. 106 Raspberry cased lamp with veins of silver throughout base and shade. Applied clear glass feet. Upturned ruffled shade. Kosmos Brenner burner. 9¼ inches high. $1800.00 VR *Hulsebus collection.*

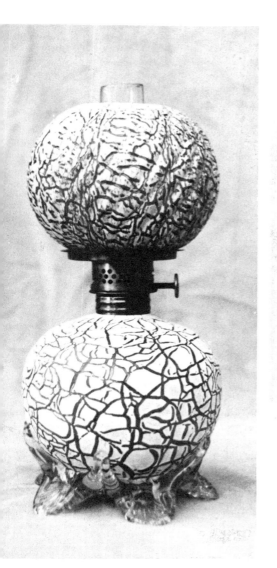

Fig. 107 Rose colored crackled overlay glass lamp with clear applied shell feet. Nutmeg burner. 9 inches high. $2000.00 VR *Hulsebus collection.*

Fig. 108 Silver pedestal lamp. Pink Nailsea font and shade, upturned fluted shade. Foreign burner. 10¼ inches high. $2000.00 VR *Hulsebus collection.*

Fig. 109 Pale pink satin glass lamp with rust colored leaves and green reeds on both shade and base. Similar to Fig. 572 in book I. Foreign burner. 6¾ inches high. $1450.00 R *Hulsebus collection.*

Fig. 110 Fireglow satin glass lamp, decorated with olive green leaves and stems, tiny white flowers. Sparr Brenner burner. 7 inches high. $2500.00 VR *Hulsebus collection.*

Fig. 111 Mother-of-pearl satin glass lamp apricot color shading to light pink. Base and shade ribbing going one direction. Satin swirl going opposite direction. Applied frosted feet. Kosmos Brenner burner. 10 inches high. $3000.00 VR *Hulsebus collection.*

Fig. 112 Rainbow Mother-of-pearl Diamond Quilted with upturned fluted shade. The font fits into a silver embossed chalice. Foreign burner. 10¼ inches high. $3500.00 VR *Hulsebus collection.*

Fig. 113 Diamond Quilted Mother-of-Pearl satin glass. Blue shading to lighter tones, decorated with coralene seaweed pattern. Ornate brass footed base. Bottom of lamp base marked "PATENT." Believed to be Webb. Kosmos burner. 9½ inches high. $4700.00 VR *Hulsebus collection.*